American Sign Language for Beginners

Complete Guide to Learn ASL in 30 days

Signing basics with clear illustrations

and comprehensive explanations

CONTENTS

Introduction

What is the nature of American Sign Language and how is it distinct from other sign languages?

American Sign Language (ASL) is a visually based natural language with similar linguistic properties to spoken English, but with a unique grammatical structure. It conveys information through sight, utilizing gestures, facial expressions, and body language. ASL is predominantly used in the Deaf communities in the USA and English-speaking parts of Canada. However, it might not be understood by people in countries like Great Britain or Australia, even though they speak English, because each country has its distinct sign language. There is no universal sign language, and within the same country, there can be different dialects based on region or ethnic group.

A notable distinction of ASL from other English-based sign languages (such as those used in Great Britain, Australia, New Zealand) is its method of fingerspelling using only one hand, a feature derived from French Sign Language, from which ASL evolved.

Why is learning American Sign Language (ASL) significant, and who is the target audience for this book?

Learning ASL is evidently crucial for the deaf and hard of hearing, as well as their friends and family. However, it's also beneficial for hearing individuals. As one of the most widely used sign languages globally and the sixth most used language in the USA, according to Gallaudet University, ASL offers the opportunity to communicate with a broad spectrum of Deaf individuals and others with disabilities. It's an effective and inclusive way to interact.

But the benefits extend beyond this.

Career Opportunities

Proficiency in ASL can be advantageous in various sectors, including public service, social work, education, healthcare, and law enforcement. It opens doors to specialized careers like interpreting or translating between English and ASL.

Communicating with Infants

Sign language can be a valuable tool for communicating with infants. Research indicates that infants as young as eight months can learn simple signs to express basic needs, potentially reducing stress for both children and parents.

Brain Development

Learning additional languages, including ASL, enhances cognitive abilities, creativity, and can help prevent dementia. ASL, in particular, offers unique benefits such as improved peripheral vision and spatial awareness, essential for mathematics and art. It also sharpens reaction times, listening skills, understanding of non-verbal cues, and fine motor skills. Essentially, ASL not only makes individuals more intellectually agile but also improves overall communication abilities.

Book 1: ASL grammar

Treat the study of American Sign Language (ASL) with the same seriousness and expectations as any spoken foreign language. Its key components include hand movements, shapes, facial expressions, and lip patterns, all of which contribute to conveying messages.

Sign language is a vital communication tool in deaf communities, with many individuals who have hearing loss being raised using sign language to interact with their families and friends. However, it's also an enriching language for those without hearing challenges to learn, offering a unique and expressive mode of communication.

ASL is predominantly used in the United States and Canada, while other countries like Malaysia, Germany, Austria, Norway, and Finland have their own versions of sign language.

Chapter 1: Mimicry

Mimicry is crucial in ASL. Deaf individuals rely on them to gauge the tone of a conversation or topic. These expressions add depth to sign language. Embrace expressing your thoughts as demonstrated by your instructor. Mimicry and other non-hand signals set ASL apart from spoken English. Non-manual signals (NMS), which include elements other than hand signs, play a significant role. For instance, adverbs in ASL are expressed using the eyes and eyebrows, while adjectives involve the mouth, tongue, and lips. Among these NMSs, facial expressions are key, serving as the tone of your "voice" in signing. Ensure your facial expressions align with your message - if you sign "I am happy," your expression should be joyful! The meaning of a sign can change with a shift in facial expression, even if the hand sign remains the same. Think of facial expressions as a spectrum, each adding a layer of meaning, much unlike English, which uses distinct words to convey related meanings.

Terrified

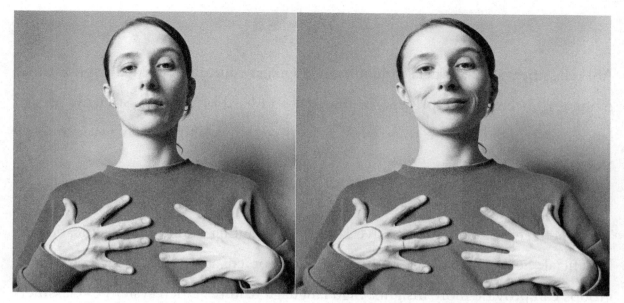

No meaning   **Not scared at all**

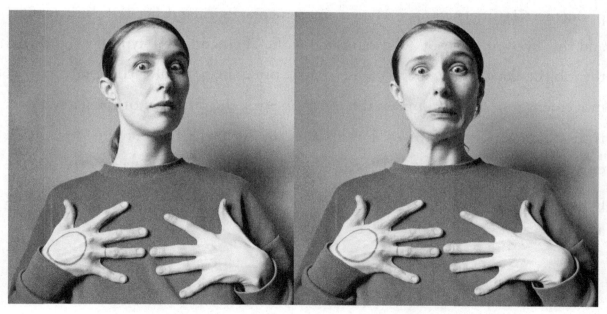

Scared   **Very scared**

ASL classifiers play a crucial role in sign language education, particularly for those training to become interpreters for the deaf and hard of hearing. Students of sign language frequently share their work related to ASL classifiers on platforms like YouTube.

To effectively learn this expressive language, acquiring additional qualifications is beneficial. Seeking guidance from instructors or engaging with deaf community groups can provide more insights. Sign language features a rich system of classifiers integral to its grammatical framework. Each classifier's morpheme includes a single phoneme. Classifiers comprise two main elements: the "handshape of the classifier" and the "movement root" it's associated with. The handshape typically represents the object, its surface, depth, and shape, often in a highly iconic manner. A movement root can encompass three morphemes: the direction of the path and its type, which act as path affixes. For instance, to depict a rabbit running downhill, a curved V-shaped classifier might be used, moving in a way that illustrates the rabbit's path. In contrast, if the rabbit is jumping, the movement would mimic a hopping action.

Chapter 2: Starting with the ASL Alphabet

Learning a new language often begins with mastering its alphabet, and American Sign Language (ASL) is no different. The foundational step in learning ASL involves using hand gestures for each letter, a process known as fingerspelling. While fingerspelling in ASL is mainly used for proper nouns or specific terms, it's akin to developing a unique handwriting style over time, yet remaining comprehensible to any ASL user.

You can easily find images or videos of the ASL alphabet, and I will provide some as well. Fingerspelling can be challenging, however, so here are some helpful pointers:

- Keep your hand steady at shoulder height, directly in front of you, avoiding any sideways movements.
- Avoid fingerspelling in front of your face, as facial expressions are a key component of ASL.
- Strive for fluid and continuous spelling, rather than spelling each letter in a disjointed manner.
- Accuracy in forming each letter is crucial, as even minor variations can lead to confusion.
- If you make an error, simply inform your conversation partner and restart the word.
- Embrace mistakes as part of the learning process.
- Practice by fingerspelling the English alphabet, your name, address, etc.

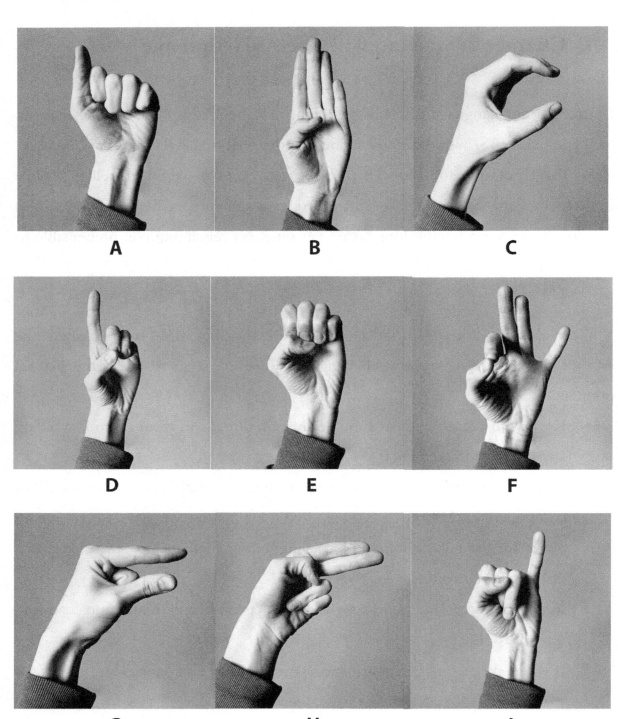

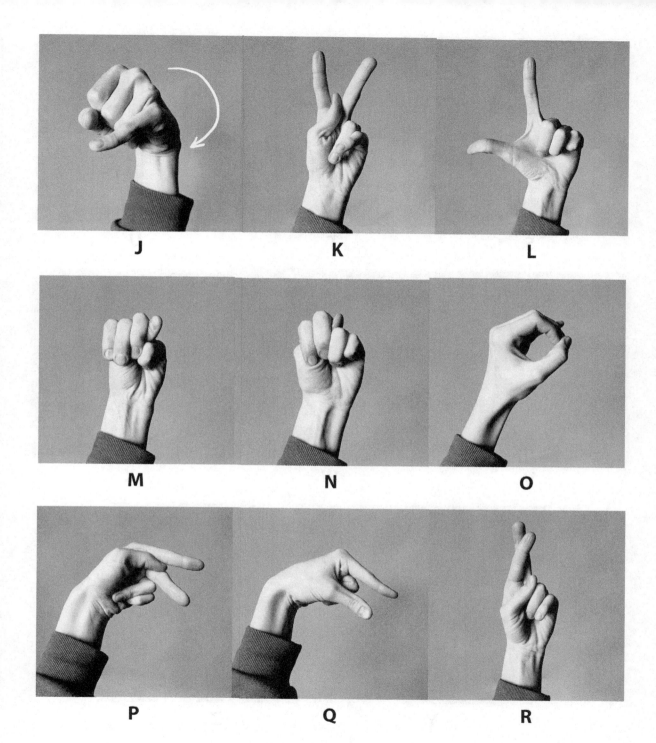

J K L

M N O

P Q R

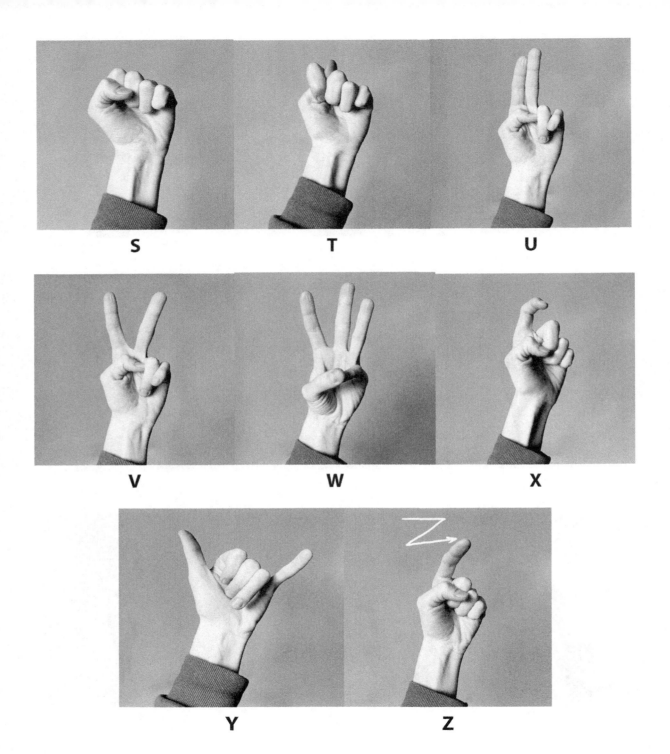

Letter A: Form a fist with the thumb positioned alongside the index finger. Ensure the thumb is visible from the viewer's perspective.

Letter B: Extend all fingers straight, keeping them together, and tuck the thumb across the palm under the fingers.

Letter C: Shape your hand to resemble a 'C'. Keep your fingers curved and the thumb in line with the fingers.

Letter D: Raise the index finger while forming a circle with the thumb and remaining fingers.

Letter E: Curl the fingertips down to the thumb, keeping the thumb positioned under the fingers.

Letter F: Touch the tip of your thumb to the tip of your index finger, creating a circle, and extend the remaining fingers.

Letter G: Extend the index and thumb fingers, positioning them to make a right angle. The rest of the fingers are curled.

Letter H: Similar to 'G', but both the index and middle fingers are extended, forming a parallel line.

Letter I: Extend the pinky finger, with the rest of the fingers curled into the palm and the thumb resting on the side.

Letter J: Make the 'I' handshape, and then move the pinky in a sweeping 'J' motion.

Letter K: Extend the index and middle fingers in a 'V' shape, and place the thumb in between, slightly touching the middle finger.

Letter L: Extend the thumb and index finger to form an 'L' shape, with the other fingers curled down.

Letter M: Tuck three fingers (index, middle, and ring) over the thumb, which is placed against the palm.

Letter N: Similar to 'M', but with only two fingers (index and middle) over the thumb.

Letter O: Make an 'O' shape by touching the fingertips to the thumb, forming a circle.

Letter P: Form a 'K' handshape and then rotate your hand so that your palm is facing outward.

Letter Q: Like 'G', but with the palm facing behind you, and the angle of the thumb and index finger pointing downwards.

Letter R: Cross your index finger over your middle finger, slightly bending both, and keep the other fingers curled.

Letter S: Make a fist with the thumb in front of the fingers, not tucked in.

Letter T: Tuck the thumb between the index and middle finger, near the top of the palm.

Letter U: Extend the index and middle fingers while keeping them together, and curl the other fingers into the palm.

Letter V: Extend the index and middle fingers away from each other to form a 'V', with the other fingers curled into the palm.

Letter W: Like 'V', but with the ring finger also extended, forming a wider shape.

Letter X: Extend the index finger and curl it slightly at the knuckle, with the other fingers curled into the palm.

Letter Y: Extend the thumb and pinky finger, keeping the other fingers curled into the palm.

Letter Z: Draw a 'Z' in the air with the index finger, or simply sign it as you would write it.

The first step in learning ASL is to get familiar with its alphabet. 'Fingerspelling' is the practice of using the ASL alphabet to spell out words. It's commonly used for proper nouns and specific items within categories. The way you form letters with your hands is unique but should follow recognizable patterns. Clarity is essential in fingerspelling to be understood. Use the correct handshapes without any approximations.

Generally, avoid a side-to-side motion of your hand like a typewriter when spelling each letter in a word. There are exceptions, like double letters, but don't focus on these initially.

Mistakes are natural. If you err in fingerspelling, don't gesture wildly as if to erase the mistake. Instead, simply shake your head and start the word over. Aim to fingerspell quickly and clearly. If unsure where to start practicing, try fingerspelling:

- Your first and last names, with a slight pause between them.
- The vowels A, E, I, O, U.
- Names of family members and friends.
- The place where you were born.
- Common letter combinations (like -sh, -ch, -th, -ck).

Learning and accurately fingerspelling the ASL alphabet is vital when starting to learn sign language, particularly for introducing yourself. Once proficient in fingerspelling, you'll need to learn to read others' fingerspelling, which can be challenging and requires practice. Don't hesitate to ask for repetition if needed.

Remember, ASL is not English. If it were, you'd already be fluent. So be patient with yourself. With dedication and practice, you'll master the ASL alphabet and fingerspelling with ease.

While ASL grammar might seem daunting at first, once you grasp the basics, you'll find yourself using sign language more naturally.

It's a common misconception that ASL is just a signed form of English. This leads to the mistaken belief that ASL and English have similar grammatical structures.

However, ASL is a distinct visual language with its own grammar and syntax. English has a linear structure with fixed word order, where changing the position of a verb or adjective can change the meaning.

Sign language grammar, in contrast, is more flexible, allowing different word orders to convey the same idea.

Chapter 3: ASL numbers

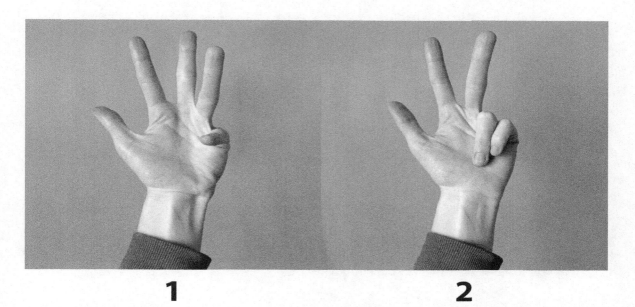

| 1 | 2 |

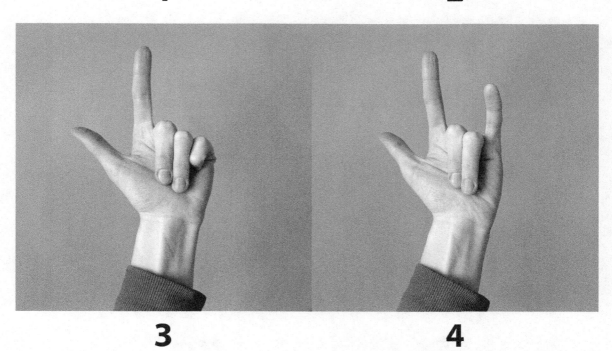

| 3 | 4 |

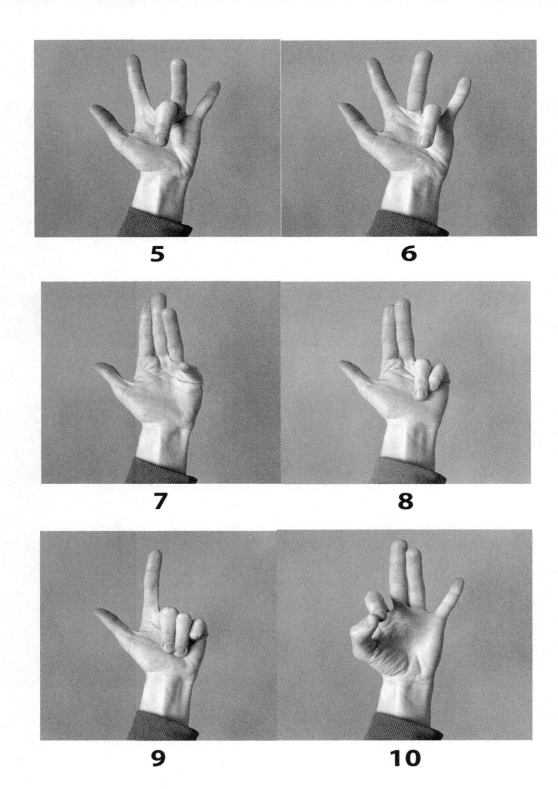

Number 1: Extend the index finger, keeping the rest of the fingers closed and the thumb alongside the palm. The palm faces outward.

Number 2: Extend the index and middle fingers, keeping them together with the other fingers closed and the thumb tucked in. The palm faces outward.

Number 3: Extend the thumb, index, and middle fingers, while keeping the ring and pinky fingers closed. The palm faces outward.

Number 4: Extend all fingers while keeping the thumb tucked in. The palm faces outward, displaying all four fingers.

Number 5: Open your hand fully with all fingers spread out and the thumb extended. The palm faces outward, resembling a 'stop' sign.

Number 6: Form a circle with the thumb and the pinky finger, extending them while keeping the other fingers closed. The palm faces outward.

Number 7: Extend the thumb, index, and middle fingers, then hook the index finger slightly. The palm faces outward, with the ring and pinky fingers closed.

Number 8: Extend the thumb and index finger, keeping them slightly apart, and fold the other fingers into the palm. The palm faces outward.

Number 9: Curl the index finger towards the palm and extend the thumb, keeping the other fingers closed. The palm faces outward.

Number 10: Extend the thumb and wave it back and forth. This sign is like a combination of '1' and '0'.

Chapter 4: ASL days of the week

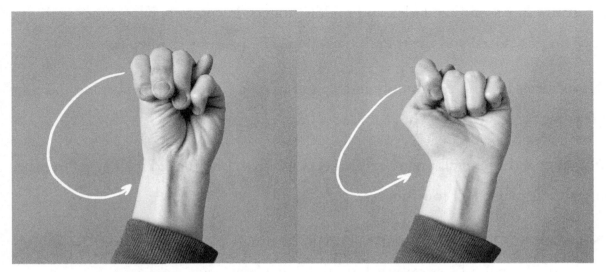

Monday　　　　**Tuesday**

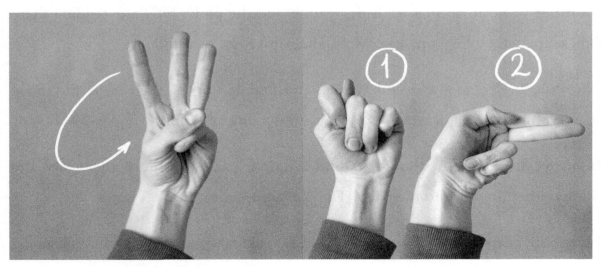

Wednesday　　　　**Thursday**

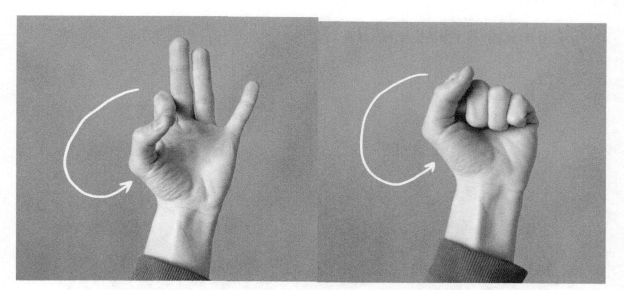

Friday   **Saturday**

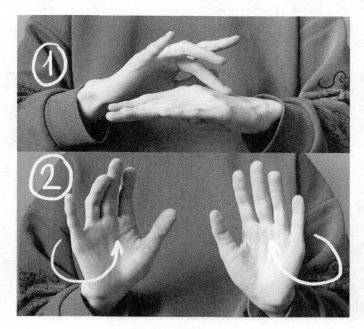

Sunday

Orange

Pink

Purple   **Purple**

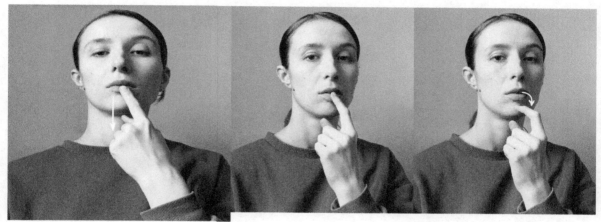

Red   **Red**

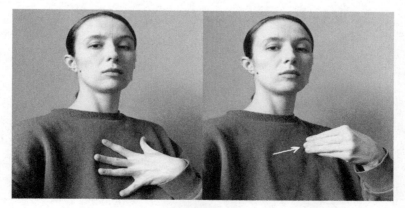

White

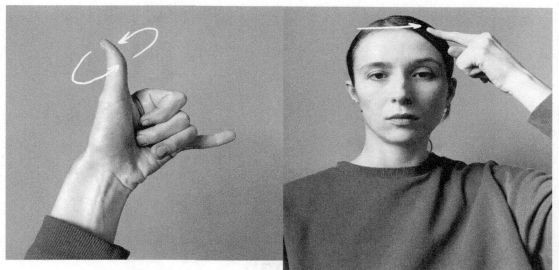

Yellow   **Black**

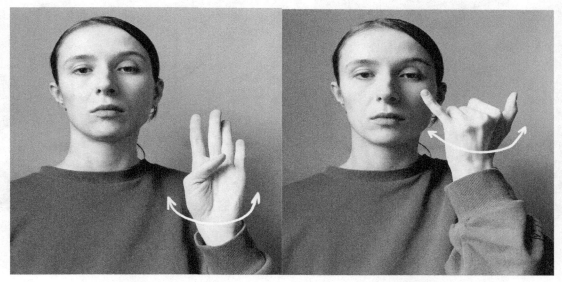

Blue   **Yellow**

25

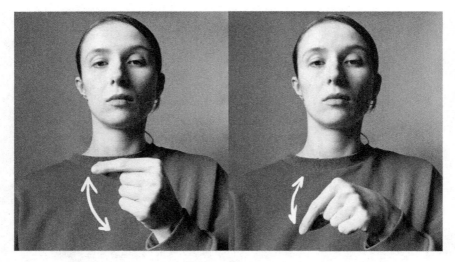

Green

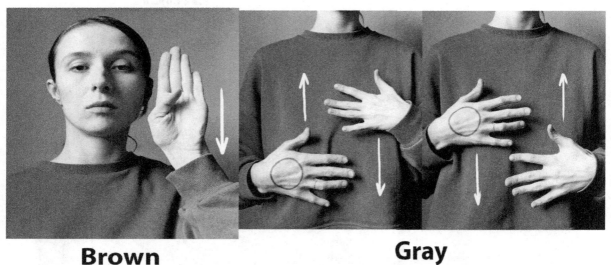

Brown   **Gray**

Orange: Start by making the handshape for the letter 'O' in ASL. This is done by touching the tip of your thumb to the tip of your index finger, forming a circle, while the other fingers are curled down.

Pink: With the 'P' handshape, bring your hand up to your chin. Brush the tip of your extended middle finger against your lower lip. This is typically done once or twice.

Purple: Start by making the handshape for the letter 'P' in ASL. This is done by making a fist, extending your index finger and thumb outward. The index finger is straight and the thumb crosses behind it, similar to the handshape for the letter 'K', but with the middle finger pointing downwards.

Red: With your index finger extended, place the tip of the finger on your lips. Then, slide the finger down your chin. This motion is typically done just once. **White:** After touching your chest, move your hand away from your chest in a forward and slightly downward motion. This movement should be smooth and gentle. It's like mimicking the action of pulling on the front of a shirt. **Yellow:** Start by making the handshape for the letter 'Y' in ASL. This is done by extending your thumb and pinky finger while keeping your other fingers curled down.

Brown: While keeping the hand in the 'B' shape and in contact with your forehead, move your hand down along the side of your face. This motion is typically done just once.

Gray: This movement is typically done in front of your chest or slightly to the side of your body.

Chapter 6: ASL Facial Expressions

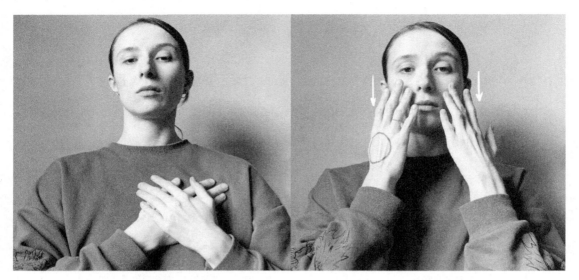

LOVE　　　　**SAD**

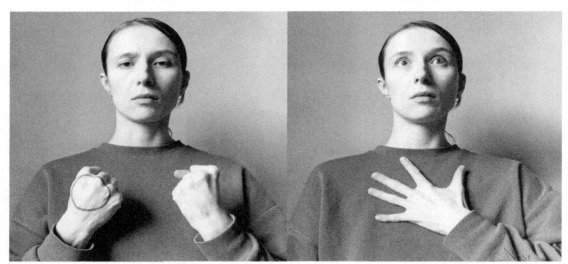

ANGRY　　　　**AFRAID**

MORE

WATER

SORRY

STOP

Love: Begin with both hands open and palms facing your body. Raise your arms and cross them over your chest, placing the palm of each hand on the opposite shoulder. It's as if you're giving yourself a hug.

Sad: Start with both hands open and palms facing inward, fingers slightly spread. Raise your hands to just below your eyes, keeping your palms facing you. Slowly move your hands downward along your face, allowing your fingers to slightly follow the contour of your face. This motion should be smooth and gentle.

Angry: Start with both hands open, palms facing down, and fingers spread apart.Place your hands in front of your chest, with the fingers spread. Your palms should still be facing downwards.Push your hands downwards in a forceful motion, bending your fingers inwards towards your palms as you do so. This movement is usually made once or twice and represents the intensity of the emotion.

Afraid: A hand with splayed fingers lies on her chest. The face depicts fright.

More: Start by making a flat 'O' shape with both hands. Do this by bringing all your fingertips together on each hand, so your hands each look like a flattened 'O' or a beak. The tips of your fingers and thumbs should be touching or nearly touching. With your hands in the flat 'O' shapes, bring your hands together and have the fingertips of each hand touch each other. Your fingers should be pointing up. Tap the fingertips of both hands together a few times. Usually, this is done two or three times.

Water: Start by making the handshape for the letter 'W' in ASL. This is done by extending your index, while keeping your thumb and little finger tucked into your palm.

Sorry: Form a Fist: Start by making a fist with your dominant hand. This means curling your fingers into your palm and placing your thumb over the side of your index finger. Place the knuckles or the side of your fist (where your thumb is resting) against the middle of your chest. While keeping your fist against your chest, move it in a small circular motion a couple of times. This motion is generally done clockwise.

STOP: Start with one hand open, fingers extended and the palm facing forward. This is similar to a 'stop' gesture used in everyday non-verbal communication.
Facial expressions are a key component in the syntax of sign language, with our eyebrows playing a crucial role in framing our sentences.

In English, transforming a statement into a question involves rearranging words. In ASL, word order is less significant as eyebrows are used to denote whether a sentence ends with a question mark, exclamation point, or period.

For questions like WHO, WHAT, WHERE, WHEN, WHY, and WHICH, we lower our eyebrows to denote curiosity or inquiry. For YES or NO questions, we raise our eyebrows.

Facial expressions in ASL also serve to express emotions. When signing emotions like HAPPY, SAD, or MAD, it's essential to match the facial expression to the sign. Hence, signing HAPPY with a sad face is grammatically incorrect in ASL.

Moreover, facial expressions in ASL are used to add emphasis, similar to how we use the word "very" in English to stress the importance of a statement. In ASL, we use facial expressions instead of an additional sign for this purpose.

Another parallel between ASL and English is the use of tone, which is the third function of facial expressions in ASL. Consider the different meanings conveyed by the word "fine" based on tone, like contentment, frustration, or anger.

In ASL, tone is communicated through facial expressions and the manner in which the sign FINE is executed. This could involve enlarging the sign, shortening its duration, or modifying its movement to reflect the intended tone.

Body Movement in ASL Grammar

Body movement is as crucial as facial expressions in the grammar of sign language. It includes any extra motion accompanying a sign.

Take the sign for UNDERSTAND, for example. Touch your forehead with your index finger resting on your thumb pad, and then flick the index finger upward.

Surprisingly, the sign for DON'T UNDERSTAND is the same, but with a crucial difference: it includes a head shake. By shaking our head from side to side while signing, we change both the syntax and the meaning of the message.

Understanding Concepts in ASL

ASL, like any language, uses gestures to convey meanings and concepts, not just words. A single sign in ASL can have multiple English interpretations, and one sign can often represent a whole English sentence.

For example, the direction of the sign ASK indicates who is being asked. "I ask her" and "she asks me" can be represented with the same sign ASK, differing only in the direction of your palm.

You can also express "I asked her repeatedly" using just the ASL sign for ASK, by repeating the sign in the same direction, whereas in English, this would require several words.

ASL also doesn't use English words like "and," "or," "the," "of," and "is." Instead, these concepts are conveyed through facial expressions, role shifts, and pointing.

Classifiers in ASL

The concept of classifiers might initially seem daunting to ASL learners. However, understanding and using classifiers can significantly enhance your signing abilities. Classifiers are essential for storytelling in sign language; without them, your ability to convey narratives is limited.

What are classifiers in ASL?

A classifier (CL) in sign language is a sign that categorizes nouns or referents into groups. It indicates the class a noun belongs to.

For example, a "horizontal 3-handshape" classifier can represent various vehicles like cars, trucks, bicycles, motorcycles, or submarines.

Classifiers are often used alongside verb/noun phrases, functioning similarly to pronouns in predicates. Like pronouns, a noun's classifier must be established before it can be used as a reference. A classifier's handshape can be combined with movements, palm orientations, and/or locations to convey more information.

Classifiers are not unique to sign language; some spoken languages use grammatical methods to categorize noun referents, though their systems have distinct characteristics.

Classifiers in Sign Language

Classifiers in sign language are handshapes used to represent different classes of nouns or referents. Here are some common classifiers:

- **CL:1** Classifier Handshape "1": This upright index finger handshape (CL1) is often used to represent thin or tall objects or people, like a human, twig, pole, pen, or stick. Remember, the specific noun should be signed before using its classifier in a sentence.

- **CL:2** Two-Claw Classifier Handshape: When held horizontally (except for representing something upside down), this handshape can depict a group of items, such as animals, chairs, toilets, rocking chairs, or a person sitting.

- **CL:B** Classifier Handshape "B" (Open Thumb): This handshape is commonly used to signify flat objects like paper, tables, and beds. When held upright, it can refer to a picture, a wall, or similar structures.

Expanding the Use of Classifiers

Classifiers go beyond mere handshapes; they also incorporate elements like location, palm orientation, and movement to convey more nuanced information.

For example, a signer might use the ASL word for 'table' and then use a classifier (palm down) to represent the table. This often involves using the passive (non-dominant) hand for the classifier while the dominant hand signs the next noun, like 'CAT'.

Representation of 'Cat' in American Sign Language

In ASL, to signify 'cat', the signer uses one hand to form the noun 'cat' and immediately applies a classifier (CL:2 claw). The classifier for the table (passive hand) is maintained throughout this signing.

The 2-claw classifier symbolizes the cat. This combination of nouns and classifiers can convey different scenarios involving the cat. For instance:

- 'CAT-ON-TABLE' means "the cat is on the table."
- 'LAYING-DOWN-ON-TABLE' implies "the cat is lying down on the table."

The signer alters the palm orientation of the classifier to represent a cat lying down. If the signer lowers her eyes while signing 'laying down', it suggests "the cat is reclining on the table." If the sign for 'lying down' is done with the eyes closed, it indicates the cat is asleep.

Using classifiers effectively in sentences is crucial in ASL. The more you understand and utilize classifiers, the more you'll enjoy and enrich your communication in sign language. Classifiers add depth and variety to the expressive capabilities of sign language.

Chapter 7: Understanding ASL Grammar

Let's delve into some fundamental aspects of sign language grammar. Note that ASL isn't written and isn't English, so when we write the signs, we use "ASL gloss," representing the signs in English words written in capital letters.

ASL Sentence Construction

In ASL grammar, there are two primary sentence structures:

> Time + Topic + Comment + Referent
>
> Topic + Comment + Referent

In these sentence structures:

- "Time" indicates when something is happening, similar to the present tense.
- "Topic" is about the subject of the sentence.
- "Comment" is what is being said about the topic.
- "Referent" pertains to the person or thing being discussed.

Let's restructure a simple English sentence into ASL. We'll use the sentence: "I'm leaving for vacation tomorrow."

In ASL, this sentence breaks down into:

- Tomorrow as the time.
- Vacation as the topic.
- 'Go' as the comment.
- 'I' as the referent.

Thus, in ASL, you would sign: "Tomorrow vacation, I go."

Notice the difference in language structure? The word "going" is reduced to GO. In ASL, the same signs are used regardless of tense, so we use the basic, unconjugated form of verbs when constructing the sentence.

The tense of the verb GO is implied by the time indicator, like TOMORROW, YESTERDAY, TODAY, SUNDAY, or NEXT WEEK. Hence, the time element should always be at the beginning of an ASL sentence.

Advanced tip: When asking a question in ASL, the interrogative words WHO, WHAT, WHERE, WHEN, WHY, and WHICH are typically placed at the end of the sentence (or sometimes at both the beginning and end).

Book 2: How to practice ASL?

Chapter 8: Understanding Hand Placement in ASL

Knowing the correct position for your hands is crucial in ASL. Typically, your palm should face your conversation partner. Keep your hand at chest level with a bent elbow for visibility and clarity of signs.

Practice at a Steady Pace

When learning, take it slow and steady. This approach helps refine your movements and makes it easier for others to understand your signing.

Master the Manual Alphabet

The manual alphabet is essential for spelling out words you don't know the signs for, even though it's not frequently used in regular conversation. Consult a manual to learn the specific handshapes for each letter.

Expand Your Vocabulary Gradually

Starting with the alphabet is great, but remember, most communication in ASL is through phrases. Enhance your vocabulary by learning new words and phrases you encounter. Like any language, constant practice and vocabulary expansion are key to proficiency.

Invest in a Quality Sign Language Dictionary

A comprehensive dictionary is vital for learning any language, including ASL. It's invaluable for looking up unfamiliar gestures and adding to your learning resources.

Effective Strategies to Learn ASL

Wondering about the best methods to learn ASL? Here are some effective tips to boost your ASL skills quickly and make learning more engaging:

Learn the Top 100 Most Useful Vocabulary

Start with basic phrases like "hello," "thank you," and "please." Once you know a few words, you can begin to communicate in ASL.

Familiarize Yourself with the Fingerspelling Alphabet

Learning the ASL alphabet is a foundational step. It enables you to spell out any word, so if you forget a sign, you can always spell it. Practice spelling everyday objects around you, such as C-O-M-P-U-T-E-R or T-R-E-E.

Learn the Phrase "How do I sign..."

Once you're comfortable with fingerspelling and can ask, "How do I sign... (spelled word)?" you'll be equipped to inquire about any sign. So, focus on mastering this useful phrase.

Chapter 9: Jumping into Conversations

Start engaging in conversations and signing as soon as possible! With a few basic words and the alphabet under your belt, don't hesitate to interact with other ASL users. Communication is essential in language learning, and many learners mistakenly postpone this step.

Join the Local Deaf Community or Find a Practice Partner

To converse, you need partners. Look for a Deaf community in your area and attend their events to immerse yourself in signing. If you're in a remote area, seek online practice partners, like in Facebook groups, and use video calls for interaction.

Don't Worry About Understanding Everything

It's common for language learners to fear not grasping everything in a conversation. Focus on the general idea rather than every sign. Your understanding will grow over time, and things will become clearer.

People are generally understanding and will help you if you're struggling to understand a sign.

Learn Common Phrases

Familiarize yourself with key phrases that matter to you. This enhances fluency, especially in casual conversations.

Expect Fluctuations in Learning

Remember, everyone has off days. There will be times when you feel you're not progressing. Don't let this discourage you; learning isn't always a straight path. It's often challenging, but your skills will improve with time.

Establish Good Habits

Consistency is key in learning ASL. Practice daily, even if it's just for 5-10 minutes. Keeping up a regular routine is more important than the length of each session.

Embrace Mistakes

Children often learn faster because they're not afraid to make mistakes. Mistakes are a crucial part of learning. Be less self-conscious and embrace a more playful, child-like approach to learning. People are generally not judgmental.

Apply Pareto's Principle

The Pareto principle, or the 80/20 rule, suggests that 20% of your learning contributes to 80% of your progress in ASL. Focus on engaging with the language through listening, reading, and speaking, rather than getting bogged down in grammar details or rare words.

Find Your Favorite ASL YouTuber

Immerse yourself in ASL through social media. Find channels that interest you and make learning more enjoyable.

Track Your Progress

Record your progress to stay motivated. Weekly videos of your signing are great for this. You can keep them private or share them online as a testament to your journey.

Set Goals

Setting daily, weekly, or monthly goals can keep you motivated. For example:

- Learn five signs a day.
- Have one sign language conversation a week.
- Learn twenty phrases a month.

Keep It Fun and Remember Your Why

The most important tip is to enjoy learning ASL. If it's not fun, your motivation might dwindle. Also, keep in mind why you're learning sign language. Your personal reason will drive you to continue.

Top Apps for Learning ASL

Communication, often taken for granted, is an essential aspect of human interaction, crucial for expressing thoughts, feelings, and desires. It plays a key role in self-esteem and building relationships. For those who cannot speak verbally, like the deaf community, American Sign Language (ASL) is vital. For those looking to learn ASL, numerous apps are now readily available.

Chapter 10: List of some of the best ASL apps currently available

- SignSchool – Great for both learning and expanding your sign language vocabulary. SignSchool is versatile, accessible on Android, Apple devices, or computers.
- ASL Dictionary – For a one-time fee of $5, this app offers a comprehensive reference for ASL, with video clips for signs. It's available for Apple and Android devices and can be used offline.
- ASL Coach – Free for iPad and iPhone users (with in-app purchases), ASL Coach is ideal for beginners. It offers an easy way to learn the sign language alphabet and comes with instructional videos.
- Mimix3D Sign Language – This Android app translates spoken and written English into ASL using a 3D avatar. It's a helpful tool for real-time communication with the deaf community.
- ASL with Care Bears – Targeted at young learners, this iPhone app (free with a premium version available) makes learning sign language fun with the Care Bears, teaching various common phrases.

Best Online ASL Classes & Courses of 2024

For those seeking top-notch online ASL classes in 2024, there's a wide range of courses taught by experienced instructors. These courses not only teach ASL but also provide insights into deaf culture and community.

From ASL basics to advanced conversational skills and storytelling, these online courses cater to a variety of learners, including homeschoolers, college students, and adults. Let's dive into the world of ASL learning!

American Sign Language Level 1 on Skillshare

Kicking off my list is an outstanding course on Skillshare by Manny Martin from The Intellezy Trainers. This course lays the groundwork for ASL learning, providing a solid introduction to the language, its history, and the field of deaf education.

Topics covered include the alphabet, numbers 1-100, colors, animals, food and drink, verbs, emotions, and storytelling techniques. By the end of the course, students should be able to convey a simple story using ASL.

Participants also get access to downloadable PDF workbooks for note-taking and tracking progress.

The course is accessible for free during the one-month trial period on Skillshare, making it an excellent, beginner-friendly option for learning ASL.

Highlights:

- 23 lessons totaling 2 hours and 14 minutes.
- Over 17,300 students enrolled.
- 97% student satisfaction rate.

American Sign Language "Basics" on Udemy

Next up is an equally impressive course by JP Cappalonga on Udemy, designed for complete beginners in ASL.

JP's lessons are followed by practical exercises to reinforce learning and build a strong foundation. The course also delves into aspects of deaf culture, including appropriate ways to get the attention of a deaf person.

Key topics include the manual alphabet, fingerspelling, numbers 1-10, greetings, colors, and basic questioning techniques.

With comprehensive content and available Levels 2 and 3, this is a highly recommended course for those serious about mastering ASL.

Features:

- Interactive exercises and quizzes.
- 4.5-star rating.
- 14 lectures over 1 hour and 51 minutes.
- Lifetime access to course materials.
- Certificate of completion included.

American Sign Language Proficiency

This course offers video demonstrations teaching the sign alphabet, names, animals, numbers, and places, covering practical scenarios like restaurant orders and directions.

Designed to build foundational skills for confident communication in sign language, this course is also a valuable asset for job seekers.

Key Points:

- Enrolled by roughly 7,000 students with a 4.6-star rating.
- Suitable for beginners.
- Provides a completion certificate.
- Highly affordable.

American Sign Language Level 1 on Udemy

This Udemy course is perfect for those looking to move beyond basic ASL and delve into more complex aspects of the language.

In this course, learners will cover ASL basics such as the alphabet, numbers 1-99, colors, animals, family members, food and drink, verbs, and emotions. This course also features practice sessions to enhance signing skills.

One drawback is the absence of subtitles, which may limit accessibility for deaf learners. Nonetheless, it serves as an excellent resource for those who are hearing and eager to learn intermediate-level ASL.

Upon completing the course, students have the option to receive a printed certificate of completion.

Highlights:

- Udemy's top-rated ASL course.
- 4.6-star rating with over 16,000 students.
- Lifetime access to course materials.
- Includes a completion certificate.

Gallaudet University: ASL Courses Online

Next, Gallaudet University offers a series of comprehensive ASL courses, consisting of four core modules. These are designed to be taken sequentially.

ASL 1 introduces beginners to deaf culture. ASL II expands on basics, covering pronominalization, classifiers, spatial referencing, pluralization, and more. ASL III focuses on narrative skills, requiring a grasp of advanced ASL vocabulary and grammar. ASL IV is the most advanced module, further expanding vocabulary and grammatical skills.

Each course costs around $300, positioning it at a higher price point but offering university-level education surpassing most community college ASL courses.

Advantages:

- High-quality, comprehensive instruction.
- Self-paced with weekly deadlines.
- Great for those aiming for proficiency in ASL.

- Interactive opportunities with the deaf community.

ASL Expressions Lessons #1-6 on Udemy

This course, taught by experienced instructor Tara Adams, includes seven lectures and takes about 1.5 hours to complete. Each lesson comes with a printable PDF for easy reference and study.

By the end of this course, students will be able to engage in basic ASL conversations, introduce themselves, respond to questions, and ask about unknown signs.

Participants will learn over 120 signs, 60 phrases, fingerspelling, basic ASL grammar, and important aspects of deaf and ASL culture.

Key Features:

- Short duration: 7 lectures, 1 hour and 35 minutes.
- Downloadable materials provided.
- Suitable for beginners with no prerequisites.
- Lifetime access to course materials.
- Certificate of completion included.

Begin ASL Online Courses

Start ASL offers three online courses: Start ASL 1, 2, and 3, each building on the previous. ASL 1 is suitable for beginners, while ASL 3 leads to fluent ASL communication.

ASL 1 covers fingerspelling, numbers, sign parameters, sentence patterns, pronouns, verbs, identifying people, plus deaf culture and history. It includes over 550 vocabulary and phrase videos across 60 lessons.

ASL 2 deepens understanding of sentence types, time concepts, classifiers, pluralization, and spatial aspects, including descriptions of rooms, objects, and places.

ASL 3 enhances storytelling skills, including role-shifting, conveying information, and interpreting literature and songs. It offers over 500 vocabulary and phrase videos.

Advantages:

- Courses cater to beginners, intermediates, and advanced learners.
- Mobile-friendly, self-paced structure.
- Verified completion certificates.
- Access to an ASL learning community on Facebook for networking and information exchange.

The Complete Online American Sign Language Course by Sign Language 101

Sign Language 101's course allows you to learn ASL at your own pace. It systematically covers vocabulary, numbers, ASL learning strategies, and insights into Deaf culture. To enhance your skills, the course includes 50 receptive practice questions and 100 fingerspelling exercises.

Dr. Byron W. Bridges, an accomplished author, educator, and lecturer with over 30 years of experience, leads the course. Born deaf to deaf parents and growing up with a deaf sister, Dr. Bridges has primarily used American Sign Language throughout his life. His educational background includes a BA in Deaf Studies from California State University, Northridge, an MA in Linguistics from Gallaudet University, and a doctorate in Deaf Studies and Deaf Education from Lamar University. He also holds a Certified Deaf Interpreter (CDI) credential from the Registry of Interpreters for the Deaf.

This comprehensive course goes beyond the basics of the alphabet, numbers, and colors to include everyday vocabulary, hobbies, directions, and sports. Over eight and a half hours, learners will acquire 1400 essential vocabulary words. It's recommended to spend a minimum of ten weeks on Level 1 and Level 2, to properly practice and benefit from the more than one hundred well-designed learning exercises.

Book 3: Deaf community

Chapter 11: Deaf Culture and Community Involvement

Deaf culture encompasses the entirety of the deaf community's life experiences. This includes tackling issues like audism and participating in artistic expressions, offering opportunities for everyone to engage.

The roots of Deaf culture in America trace back to 1817 at the American School for the Deaf in Connecticut. Deaf American identity represents those who belong to the linguistic minority of American Sign Language users. This includes not only those who are medically deaf but also some hearing individuals proficient in ASL. The term encompasses those with hearing loss who primarily communicate using ASL.

In Deaf culture, terms like "deaf" and "hard of hearing" are embraced positively, reflecting a strong sense of identity and pride. The use of 'Deaf' with a capital 'D' refers to individuals who identify primarily with the Deaf community, while 'deaf' with a lowercase 'd' indicates a hearing impairment.

Advocacy in the Deaf and Hard of Hearing Community

The deaf and hard of hearing community has a rich history of activism. Notably, students at Gallaudet University have led significant protests, such as the "Deaf President Now" movement in the 1980s, which resulted in the appointment of the university's first deaf president. Another major protest, "Unity for Gallaudet," occurred in the early 2000s, focusing on presidential selection and academic issues.

Developments in Assistive Technology

Assistive technologies for the deaf and hard of hearing have a long history. Today, these technologies enable people to use phones and watch TV programming.

Closed captioning, though it seems longstanding, is relatively new. It started with open captioning in 1972 and became more accessible after the 1996 Telecom Act mandated its inclusion.

The development of cochlear implants, beginning with early experiments in 1790, gained momentum in the late 20th century. By 1984, the technology was no longer considered experimental and has rapidly advanced since.

Hearing aids have evolved significantly, from early ear trumpets to modern behind-the-ear devices. Technologies like text messaging, Skype, and email have eased communication challenges, but before these, the TTY, invented by Robert Weitbrecht, was a vital tool, with its first long-distance call in 1964.

Chapter 12: Economic Challenges in the Deaf and Hard of Hearing Community

Historically, economic survival for the deaf and hard of hearing community has been fraught with challenges. During the Great Depression in the 1930s, deaf individuals faced similar, if not greater, hardships. A common memory from this era includes "deaf peddlers," who sold alphabet cards for income.

Deaf Education History

Deaf education in the U.S. has deep roots, dating back to the 19th century. A significant setback occurred during the Second International Congress on Deaf Education in Milan in 1880, where a resolution was passed banning sign language use, opposed only by the U.S. and the U.K.

Segregation was also an issue in deaf schools, mirroring the segregation in public schools, with black deaf students barred from attending classes with white deaf students.

Despite these challenges, institutions like Gallaudet University have evolved from their beginnings in deaf education to become prominent centers for learning and advocacy.

Media Evolution in the Deaf Community

Media representation for the deaf and hard of hearing community has seen remarkable progress, paralleling advancements in technology and education. The rise of deaf-focused media outlets began with publications like the now-discontinued "Silent News." Television has featured deaf characters for years, and there have been initiatives to establish deaf-specific cable channels. The internet has revolutionized accessibility, offering a modern platform akin to a deaf cable channel.

Notable Figures in Deaf History

Throughout history, many deaf and hard of hearing individuals, along with some hearing allies, have significantly contributed to deaf culture and history. For instance, a deaf person created the popular Girl Scout cookies. In the 19th century, a deaf woman made her mark as a journalist. The history is rich with notable deaf figures, including Helen Keller, Thomas Edison, and Laura Redden Searing.

Origins of Sign Language

The history of sign language often intrigues students. While the deaf educator Abbé de l'Épée of France is commonly recognized for developing an early form of sign language that influenced ASL, the origins trace back to Pierre Desloges, another deaf author from France.

Chapter 13: Challenging Times in Deaf History

The resurgence of interest in American Sign Language (ASL) in the mid-20th century marked a significant turning point. Scholars and educators began to recognize the linguistic validity and richness of ASL. One pivotal figure in this shift was William Stokoe, a professor at Gallaudet University. In the 1960s, Stokoe's groundbreaking research demonstrated that ASL was a true language with its own syntax, grammar, and structure, not merely a collection of gestures or a simplified version of English.

Stokoe's work helped to change perceptions about ASL and Deaf culture. It laid the groundwork for ASL to be recognized and studied as a legitimate language, which had profound implications for Deaf education and the Deaf community. This recognition played a crucial role in the revival of sign language in educational settings.

By the late 20th and early 21st centuries, the Deaf community witnessed significant advancements. ASL was increasingly incorporated into public schools and higher education institutions. Deaf studies and interpreter training programs became more widespread, and ASL classes were offered not only to Deaf students but also to hearing students, further promoting awareness and understanding of Deaf culture.

Technological advancements also played a role in the spread and acceptance of ASL. The internet and social media platforms allowed for greater visibility of sign language and Deaf culture. Online resources made learning ASL more accessible to a broader audience, and video technology facilitated communication within the Deaf community and between Deaf and hearing individuals.

In the realm of law and policy, there were significant strides as well. Legislation such as the Americans with Disabilities Act (ADA) of 1990 provided greater accessibility and rights protection for the Deaf community, recognizing the importance of ASL as a means of communication. This legal recognition further validated ASL and helped to dismantle previous stigmas attached to its use.

The journey of ASL and the Deaf community is a testament to the resilience and determination of those who fought to preserve their language and culture. Today, ASL is not only recognized as a rich, complex language but also celebrated as a crucial aspect of cultural diversity in the United States. The language continues to evolve, and its study offers valuable insights into the nature of human communication and the importance of linguistic diversity.

The history of ASL and the Deaf community's struggle and triumph is a powerful reminder of the importance of preserving linguistic and cultural identities. It stands as a shining example of how understanding and embracing diversity can lead to a more inclusive and enriched society.

Conclusion

Based on my experience and insights from others, here are the advantages of learning sign languages for hearing individuals:

- Improved Communication Skills: Learning sign language enhances your ability to communicate non-verbally. It develops an awareness of body language and facial expressions, which are essential components of effective communication.

- Cultural Enrichment and Inclusivity: It provides an opportunity to engage with Deaf culture, fostering a greater understanding and appreciation of this community. This can lead to more inclusive attitudes and behaviors.

- Cognitive Benefits: Studies suggest that learning sign language can improve spatial awareness, visual sensitivity, and memory. It's a form of bilingualism, which has been linked to cognitive advantages such as enhanced multitasking and problem-solving skills.

- Career Enhancement: Proficiency in sign language can open up career opportunities, particularly in fields like education, healthcare, social work, and interpretation. It's a valuable skill that can set you apart in the job market.

- Helps in Noisy Environments or When Maintaining Silence: Sign language can be an effective mode of communication in environments where speaking isn't possible or practical – for instance, in loud settings or situations requiring silence.

- Strengthening Diverse Relationships: Learning sign language allows you to communicate with Deaf and hard-of-hearing individuals, widening your social circle and fostering relationships that might not have been possible otherwise.

- Enhanced Attention to Detail: Since sign language is visually based, it requires and thus enhances attention to detail and sharpens observational skills.

- Emergency Preparedness: Knowing sign language can be crucial in emergency situations where verbal communication isn't possible, enabling you to assist or communicate with Deaf individuals effectively.

- Boosts Sensory Awareness and Reflexes: Communicating through sign language enhances hand-eye coordination and sharpens reflexes due to the physical nature of the language.

- Personal Satisfaction and Achievement: Learning a new language, including sign language, can be a rewarding experience. It provides a sense of achievement and personal growth.

Learning any language stimulates and exercises the brain, and sign languages are no exception. They can enhance cognition, creative thinking, brain function, memory, spatial awareness, and mental rotation skills. Like riding a bike, once learned, it's a skill you won't forget.

Sign language is more prevalent than many realize. It's often overlooked how extensively people use their local sign language. Even if not immediately visible, sign language conversations are happening all around us.

In the United States, American Sign Language ranks as the third most studied modern/foreign language in colleges and universities, according to the Modern Language Association. It's also one of the most widely used languages in the country, following English and Spanish. Many might not consider sign language as a "competitor" to spoken languages, but it certainly is. The Deaf community is present globally and often goes unnoticed, yet it's all around us.

Learning a new sign language also means immersing yourself in the culture and community of the Deaf. Just like learning an oral language brings insights into a country's culture and people, learning sign language opens up the rich history and culture of the Deaf community.

You also have the chance to make new friends and connections by engaging with members of the Deaf community. If you're learning alongside others, there are opportunities to collaborate and connect, both online and offline. Many courses and workshops offer community components through dedicated Facebook Pages, allowing learners to share their experiences and journeys.

Improves Peripheral Vision and Reaction Time

A study from the University of Sheffield found that users of sign language have better peripheral vision and quicker reaction times. Due to its visual nature, learning sign language heightens awareness and enhances visual field reaction, which is beneficial in sports and driving. The researchers also noted that deaf individuals have exceptional visual abilities not typically found in hearing adults.

Sign language requires more than just observing hand movements; facial expressions, lip reading, and body language are equally important. Since you can't focus on all these elements simultaneously, peripheral vision becomes crucial and is continuously honed.

Facilitates Communication with Infants

While infants can't engage in complex conversations, basic communication through sign language is possible. This includes understanding simple signs for everyday concepts like "milk," "hungry," "sleepy," "teddy bear," "more," and "play." Infants as young as six months can start to grasp these signs. Research indicates that teaching basic signs to hearing infants can boost cognitive development and foster deeper connections between parent and child. Early exposure to multiple languages, including sign language, also prepares the brain for learning additional languages later.

Interaction with Animals

Indeed, animals can be part of the conversation too! While it's not about having full-blown conversations with pets, it's worth noting that animals, like humans, can be deaf. Some pet owners have successfully used basic sign language to communicate with and build bonds with their deaf pets.

Enhances Communication Skills

Being fluent in sign language certainly breaks down communication barriers. Even during the learning phase, patience and persistence in communication are key. For instance, when unsure about a sign, such as "business," asking and learning from a Deaf person can be enlightening. If that's not feasible, writing down the word or using the ASL alphabet on a phone or paper is an alternative.

This approach to overcoming communication barriers not only helps in learning the language but also in understanding and empathizing with the experiences of those in the Deaf community.

Enhances Spelling Skills

Learning sign language can actually improve your spelling. While most words have specific signs, there are instances where you might not know the sign for a word or a specific name, place, product, or brand. In such cases, you'll need to fingerspell them. Being proficient in spelling is advantageous as it's necessary for fingerspelling or writing them down.

Improves Listening Skills

Communicating in sign language requires undivided attention and focus on the speaker. Maintaining eye contact is crucial, and understanding sign language isn't just about hand movements; facial expressions and body language are equally important. This heightened focus enhances your listening and observational skills.

Expands Diversity

Understanding sign language can make you more inclusive and diverse in your interactions. It enables you to communicate with the Deaf community and tackle language and communication barriers, contributing to true diversity in personal and professional environments.

Adds Value to Your Business and Creates New Opportunities

While being an interpreter is a common profession requiring sign language, even basic knowledge can significantly enhance customer service. Learning sign language also teaches you about Deaf culture and etiquette, such as maintaining eye contact and understanding the nuances of interacting with deaf individuals.

Facilitates Learning Additional Languages

Once you've learned a new language, acquiring another becomes easier. If you're already bilingual, adding sign language or other languages to your skill set can be more straightforward.

Improves Body Language Skills

Sign language involves more than hand movements. Effective communication in sign language also relies on eye contact, facial expressions, and other body language cues. Mastering these aspects of communication enhances your ability to connect with others, whether they are deaf or hearing.

Offers Versatility in Communication

Sign language can be incredibly useful in noisy environments like bars or nightclubs, where verbal communication is difficult. In such settings, sign language offers a clear and effective alternative.

Sign Language in Various Settings

Imagine being in a pub and needing to communicate with a friend across the room. With sign language, you can easily do so without having to move. Similarly, if you're scuba diving and need to communicate underwater, sign language can be incredibly effective. The need to shout over loud environments could well become a thing of the past.

Facilitating Assistance When Needed

Deaf and hard of hearing individuals often face communication challenges in a predominantly hearing world. By knowing sign language, you can step in to assist in situations like a restaurant or a store where there may be a communication gap.

In a volunteer setting or at work, if you encounter someone who is deaf and feels isolated, your ability to sign can make a significant difference in making them feel included and understood. Sign language can bridge communication gaps with deaf or hard of hearing customers or colleagues.

I trust you found value and enjoyment in reading my book. Thank you for your purchase!

Made in the USA
Columbia, SC
14 June 2024

36969786R00037